Beethoven

Für Elise

T0087616

Cover photography: Copyright © 1998 Val Corbett/Panoramic Images, Chicago
All Rights Reserved.

Project editor: Peter Pickow

Copyright © 1999 by Amsco Publications,
A Division of Music Sales Corporation, New York

Order No. AM 948651
International Standard Book Number: 0.8256.1733.2

Exclusive Distributors:
Music Sales Corporation
257 Park Avenue South, New York, NY 10010 USA
Music Sales Limited
8/9 Frith Street, London W1V 5TZ England
Music Sales Pty. Limited
120 Rothschild Street, Rosebery, Sydney, NSW 2018, Australia

Printed in the United States of America by
Vicks Lithograph and Printing Corporation

 Music Sales America

DISTRIBUTED BY

7777 W. BLUEMOUND RD. P.O. BOX 13819 MILWAUKEE, WI 53213

Für Elise

Ludwig van Beethoven

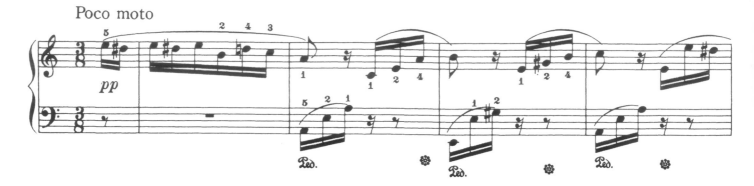

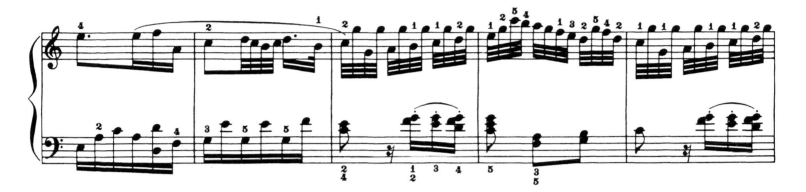

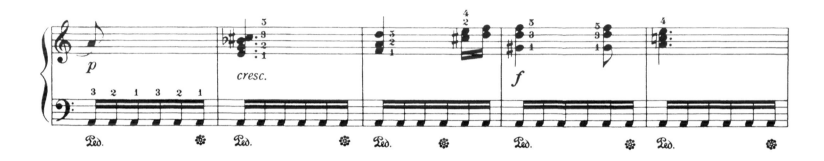

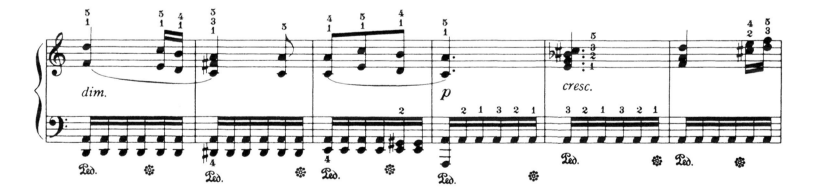

ABOUT THE CD

Your *Concert Performer* CD uses a special hybrid format to present both audio and MIDI data.

Track 1 contains an audio concert performance. This track is playable on any CD player or computer equipped with a CD-ROM drive and audio CD player software.

Track 2 is a special audio "study track," on which you'll hear the same performance as Track 1 at a slower speed. Listening to and playing along with this track can help you resolve questions of rhythm and interpretation as you are learning the piece.

MIDI data is provided for both Macintosh and IBM-compatible computers. In order to use these files, you must have software and hardware designed to play and/or edit MIDI files. The file is a Type 1 Standard MIDI File (SMF) and is completely compatible with most current hardware and software sequencers and players. The instrument assignments conform to the General MIDI Standard. The MIDI channel assignments are as follows:

MIDI Channel	Instrument
3	Piano: Right Hand
4	Piano: Left Hand

Mute one of the channels to practice one hand alone. Change the tempo or even transpose the whole piece to a new key. Add an orchestral or rock background—the possibilities are endless!

U.S. $9.99

HL14011945

Music Sales America

DISTRIBUTED BY

Hal•Leonard® CORPORATION

ISBN 978-0-8256-1733-1

50999